Blue Sharks

by Grace Hansen

Abdo
SHARKS
Kids

abdopublishing.com

Published by Abdo Kids, a division of ABDO, PO Box 398166, Minneapolis, Minnesota 55439.

Copyright © 2016 by Abdo Consulting Group, Inc. International copyrights reserved in all countries.
No part of this book may be reproduced in any form without written permission from the publisher.

Printed in the United States of America, North Mankato, Minnesota.

102016

012016

 THIS BOOK CONTAINS
RECYCLED MATERIALS

Photo Credits: Corbis, iStock, Seapics.com, Science Source, Shutterstock, Thinkstock

Production Contributors: Teddy Borth, Jennie Forsberg, Grace Hansen

Design Contributors: Laura Rask, Dorothy Toth

Library of Congress Control Number: 2015941981

Cataloging-in-Publication Data

Hansen, Grace.
 Blue sharks / Grace Hansen.
   p. cm. -- (Sharks)
ISBN 978-1-68080-151-4 (lib. bdg.)
Includes index.
1. Blue shark--Juvenile literature.   I. Title.
597.3/4--dc23
                    2015941981

Table of Contents

Blue Sharks

Blue sharks are not often seen in the wild. They live in cold and deep waters.

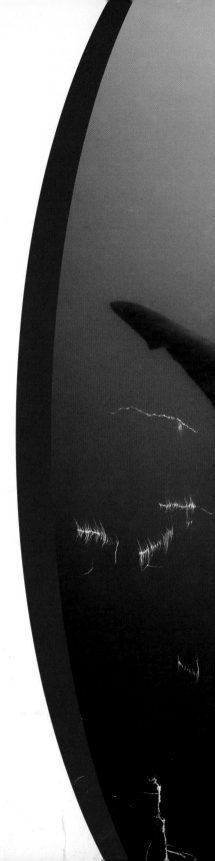

5

The blue shark has
a long nose. Its black
eyes are big and round.

The blue shark is skinnier than other shark species. Its fins look big on its thin body.

Blue sharks are good swimmers. They are some of the fastest sharks.

Food & Hunting

A blue shark's teeth are thin and sharp. Its teeth and speed make it a great hunter.

12

Blue sharks love to eat
squid. They will eat
many kinds of fish, too.

Blue sharks often live in social groups. These groups are called schools. Most other shark species live alone.

Baby Blue Sharks

Baby sharks are called **pups**.

Blue sharks can give birth

to up to 130 pups at once!

19

Pups care for themselves after birth. They will grow to about 10 feet (3 m) long.

More Facts

- People rarely see blue sharks in the wild. When blue sharks are spotted, they are often jumping out of the water. They do this to find their next meal.

- Blue sharks come in many shades of blue. They range from light blue to deep blue.

- A blue shark can sense its prey's heartbeat from miles away.

Glossary

pup – a newborn animal.

school – a group of animals that feed or migrate together.

social – a way to describe an animal that prefers to live among others of its kind, rather than alone.

Index

abdokids.com

Use this code to log on to abdokids.com and access crafts, games, videos, and more!

Abdo Kids Code:
SBK1514